Pauley & Pollyanna

Lori Josifek

WestBow Press books may be ordered through booksellers or by contacting:

WestBow Press
A Division of Thomas Nelson & Zondervan
1663 Liberty Drive
Bloomington, IN 47403
www.westbowpress.com
844-714-3454

Because of the dynamic nature of the Internet, any web addresses or links contained in this book may have changed since publication and may no longer be valid. The views expressed in this work are solely those of the author and do not necessarily reflect the views of the publisher, and the publisher hereby disclaims any responsibility for them.

Any people depicted in stock imagery provided by Getty Images are models, and such images are being used for illustrative purposes only. Certain stock imagery © Getty Images.

ISBN: 978-1-6642-6863-0 (sc)
ISBN: 978-1-6642-6864-7 (e)

Library of Congress Control Number: 2022910894

Print information available on the last page.

WestBow Press rev. date: 08/31/2022

WESTBOW
PRESS®
A DIVISION OF THOMAS NELSON
& ZONDERVAN

Dedication

To Bonnie, Lydia, Titus, Phoebe,

Madison, Elo, and Lumi ~

You keep the spark of youth lit in me,

and give me reason to write.

Dear little children, I have a true story to tell you so you might know that God is good and cares for you no matter what. Sometimes things happen that seem bad, but God is able to make something good from these things.

I know this, because God has promised that He will work all things together for good for those who love Him.

Now, Pauley and Pollyanna were pure white parakeets, which is rare for that kind of bird. They were beloved pets of a family who enjoyed breeding these friendly little birds - also called budgies. Turn the page to read their story …

God's Holy Word

Romans 8:28

And we know that all things work together for good to them that love God, to them that are the called according to His purpose.

Mr. Pearl and Sunshine, the parent parakeets, were bright blue and yellow-green colored. And right in the family's living room, in the nesting box of a large homemade cage, Mr. Pearl and Sunshine proudly watched over their five beautiful eggs.

After about three weeks, five adorable parakeets hatched from the eggs. Of course, at first, the hatchlings were pink and without feathers, but before long their white plumage appeared. Amazingly, within four or five weeks the parakeets would learn to fly.

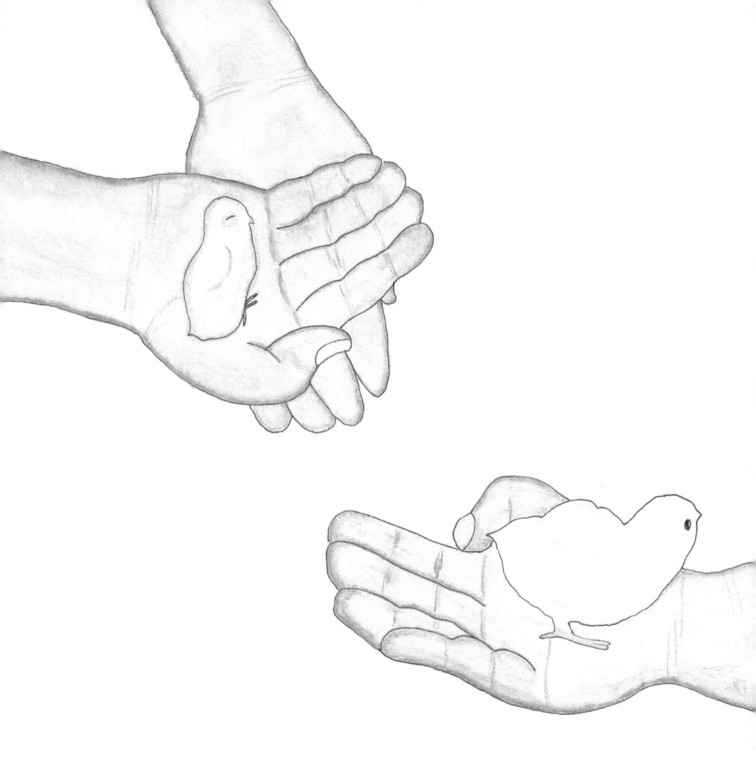

Three of these white parakeets were sold to other bird lovers, but the children wanted to keep the last two which they affectionately named Pauley and Pollyanna.

The twin birds' home was a bright yellow cage kept by a sunny window in the homeschool room. Pauley and Pollyanna made it a happy place for the children with their cheerful chirping and funny antics. Playfully, the budgies pushed each other off the perch or hung upside down from the bars like little acrobats.

11

Occasionally, the children let their budgies out of the cage to play. Pauley and Pollyanna flew around the room, landed on the ceiling fan for a merry-go-round ride, and strutted about on the desks as if they were in school.

13

Pauley and Pollyanna often landed on shoulders and lovingly pecked a kiss on the children's lips. And, there were many times the birds made the family laugh to see them curiously pecking at toys. The budgies had become members of the family and would bob or tilt their heads to communicate their happiness.

One unforgettable day, when the parakeets were out of their cage, the front door of the house had been left open and Pollyanna flew right out! To everyone's relief, she landed on a low branch of a tree right outside the door. She was easily rescued, and the family was quite careful not to repeat that scare.

Many happy months passed while the parakeets filled the home with chirping, chattering, whistling, and singing. Until one day, it was noticed that Pauley's feet looked strange. Instead of the usual soft pink, his feet were slightly purplish. The family was concerned about this and kept a close watch on Pauley's feet each day. As time went by, Pauley's feet turned a darker purplish color, and finally, they became brown and dry.

Much to the family's dismay, Pauley's feet eventually just fell off, leaving him with stubs at the end of his legs where the feet used to be. The stubs were a soft pink color indicating that Pauley was otherwise healthy. But without his feet, Pauley could no longer climb the bars or balance on the perch. It was sad for the family to see their little pet with his stubs and sitting at the bottom of the cage.

21

Pauley really wanted to be up on the perch with Pollyanna, so a small platform was attached to the perch at the side of the cage for him to sit on. The children took turns reaching into the cage and gently lifting Pauley onto his new platform whenever they noticed him at the bottom of the cage. Not long after, something truly remarkable happened.

By practicing over and over again, Pauley learned to inch his way off of the platform and onto the perch. Then he would rock back and forth until he gained his balance to sit next to Pollyanna. As the children watched in amazement, they exclaimed, "Look, Pauley's perching!"

How good it was to see the parakeets together on the perch! Pauley's triumph did not last long, though. Every time Pollyanna turned around on the perch her long tail caused Pauley to lose his balance ... and back down to the bottom of the cage he went.

In a few days, Pauley learned a new trick to get back onto the perch. The horizontal bars of the yellow cage offered the courageous little bird a way to climb back up to his sister. Pauley hooked his legs around each bar, one-by-one, until he reached the height of his platform. Once on the platform, he inched his way onto the perch where he bravely balanced himself anew. Pollyanna chirped with joy to have him back beside her, but she repeatedly knocked Pauley off the perch. He tirelessly climbed back up the bars every time and gave a happy little chirp that said, "Look at me, I did it again!"

29

Having no feet did not stop Pauley from flying. When let out of their cage, both birds happily flew around the homeschool room, even fearlessly landing on Rebel, the dog! The children were delighted to watch Pauley run across Rebel's back with his pink stubs. He didn't seem to notice that he was different from Pollyanna.

MAP OF THE WORLD

REBEL

Pauley lived for a few years after losing his feet. Pollyanna lived for sixteen years. Both were examples of God's loving care for birds - just as He has loving care for *all* creatures. But God's love and care for people is much greater, and you can be sure that no matter what happens in your life, God will take care of you.

Follow Pauley and Pollyanna to the next page to learn and sing a song that will help you to remember the wonderful truth that you can trust God to always take care of you.............

God Will Take Care of You

Be not dis- mayed— what e'er be tide;
Through days of toil— when heart doth fail,
All you may need— He will pro- vide;
No mat-ter what— may be the test,

God will take care of you.
God will take care of you.
God will take care of you.

Be- neath His wings— of love a- bide;
When dan- gers fierce— your path as- sail,
Noth- ing you ask— will be de- nied;
Lean, wea-'ry one,— up on His breast;

God will take care of you.
God will take care of you.
God will take care of you.
God will take care of you.

God will take care of you,
Through ev-'ry day o'er all the way.
He will take care— of you;
God will take care— of you.

Words by Civilla D. Martin 1904
Tune by Martin, Walter S.

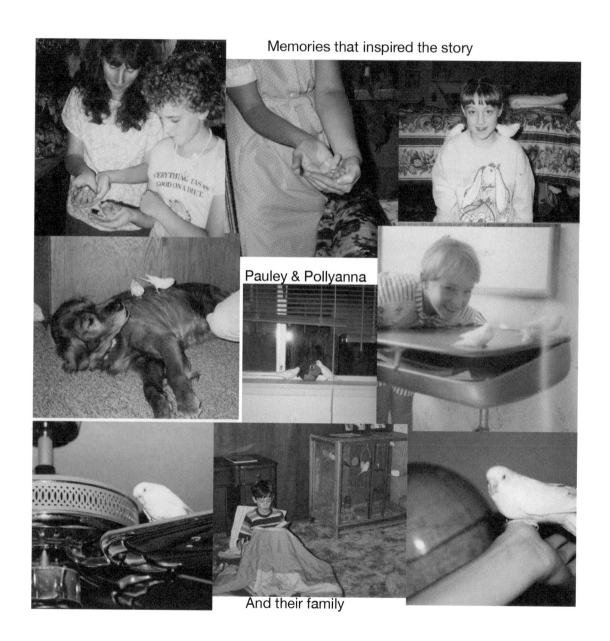

Memories that inspired the story

Pauley & Pollyanna

And their family

About the Author

Lori Josifek has worn many hats in her life as a wife, mother, grandmother, teacher, choir director, artist, and writer. Devoting her life to teaching music, writing, and poetry, among many subjects, Lori has freely spread her wealth of arts to children outside the conventional education system for more than thirty-eight years.

In her university years, Lori pursued a career in education and earned a teaching credential but did not stay in the public-school system long. After marriage and having four children, her goals refocused to providing home education to her children. Under her discipline, they earned a structured and full education beginning with music lessons around the piano every morning, Bible study and academic principles following, physical education in the afternoon, and "homework" to be completed before the next day.

During these years, Lori was inspired to start a children's choir whose presentations ministered at elderly facilities. When her children graduated on to higher education, Lori continued to teach writing classes to homeschooled children in the community.

Her writing is succinct, yet thoughtfully artistic as she paints a gentle message of her testimony of faith in her storytelling. Many of her stories and poems are inspired by her love of nature and the numerous pets who enriched her family life over the years. Lori lives in Nampa, Idaho with her husband and enjoys crocheting, camping, cooking, gardening, and spending time with her family.

Printed in the United States
by Baker & Taylor Publisher Services